ASH PACHAURI, PhD
&
SAROJ PACHAURI, MD, PhD,
DPH

Small Steps, Big Impact

*A Simple Guide to Individual Action and Collective
Impact to Tackle Climate Change*

Climate change is for real. We have just a small window of opportunity and it is closing rather rapidly. There is not a moment to lose.

Dr. Rajendra K. Pachauri

Contents

1

Understanding Climate Change

I ntroduction
    Climate change, an urgent and existential challenge of
    our time, is a global phenomenon that spares no one.
Its far-reaching consequences threaten our existence, global
economy, peace, and societal survival. In this chapter, we will
delve into the science of climate change, exploring its causes,
effects, and implications.

Understanding the Science of Climate Change
Climate change, which encompasses long-term shifts in
temperature, precipitation patterns, and other aspects of the
Earth's climatic system, is a complex phenomenon. While
natural factors such as volcanic eruptions and variations in
solar radiation have influenced climate and weather patterns
throughout history, the current nature, pace, and magnitude of
climate change, as we know it today, are primarily driven by
human activity.

The leading cause of climate change, influenced by human

activities, is the release of certain gases into the air. These gases, like carbon dioxide, methane, and nitrous oxide, trap heat from the sun in the Earth's atmosphere, leading to a warming effect known as the greenhouse effect. While some of these gases occur naturally, human activities, such as burning fossil fuels, cutting down forests, and industrial processes, have significantly increased their levels in the atmosphere, especially since the Industrial Revolution.

Consequences of Climate Change

The impacts of climate change are varied and wide-ranging, affecting the Earth's ecosystems, economies, and people world-wide. No corner of the globe is left untouched by climate change's impacts. Some of the most notable consequences include:

1. **Rising Temperatures:** Global temperatures have increased over the past century, leading to more frequent, extreme, and intense heat waves. The warming of Earth's temperatures has severe implications for human health, agriculture, water resources, food security, displacement of communities, and human security overall.
2. **Changing Weather Patterns:** Climate change has altered precipitation patterns, leading to more frequent and extreme weather events, including droughts, floods, and storms. These extreme weather events cause widespread damage to infrastructure, crops and agriculture, and environmental ecosystems.
3. **Warming of Ocean Temperatures, Melting Ice Caps, and Rising Sea Levels:** The warming climate results in sea-level rise. This poses a significant threat to coastal

ecosystems and communities due to increasing the risk of flooding and erosion.

4. **Loss of Biodiversity:** In the relentless pursuit of 'progress' through industrialization and urbanization, humans have destroyed natural plant and animal habitats through deforestation. Natural ecosystem and habitat loss have, in turn, led to shifts in and loss of flora and fauna, resulting in the permanent extinction of several species. Such biodiversity loss has cascading effects on natural ecosystem balances such as pollination, pest control, disease mitigation, and water purification.

Implications for Society

The impacts of climate change are not evenly distributed, with the most vulnerable and marginalized communities often bearing the greatest brunt of the consequences. Vulnerable populations, including low-income groups, indigenous communities, and people living in coastal or arid regions, are the most impacted and disproportionately affected by climate-related disasters and disruptions.

Furthermore, climate change exacerbates existing social and economic inequalities, creating new challenges for sustainable development and poverty alleviation efforts. Addressing climate change requires not only eliminating carbon from the atmosphere and reducing greenhouse gas emissions to mitigate the impacts of climate change but also building resilience and adaptive capacity within communities to cope with its impacts.

Conclusion

In conclusion, climate change is a complex and multifaceted

issue with far-reaching implications for the planet and all its inhabitants. Understanding the science behind climate change is essential for taking knowledge-inspired initiatives to develop effective strategies to mitigate its impacts and adapt to a changing climate. In the following chapters, we will explore the role that individuals can play by taking concrete action in their daily lives, not just to tackle the challenge of climate change but also to build a more sustainable future for future generations.

At this juncture, it's crucial to recognize that while climate change undeniably presents an existential threat to all life forms and the very existence of our planet, there exists a narrow window of opportunity for us to act and address its impacts. Nevertheless, it's imperative to acknowledge that swift action is essential, as this window is rapidly closing. Despite this urgency, as individuals, we possess the power to instigate the necessary change. By educating ourselves about our role in combatting climate change and committing to action promptly, we can seize this opportunity for transformation. History has shown that pivotal moments that reshaped the course of humanity arose from the collective efforts of individuals and society. Just as Mahatma Gandhi advocated, we have the capacity to "be the change we want to see in the world." We have done it before, and we can do it again. Considering our lives and livelihoods hinge upon it, what more significant existential challenge could unite humanity and spur us to effect change?

2

The Power of Individual Action

I ntroduction
In the face of daunting global challenges like climate change, it's easy to feel powerless as individuals. However, history has repeatedly demonstrated that individual actions can lead to significant change when magnified and multiplied. In this chapter, we will explore the power of individual action in tackling climate change and building a more sustainable future for our planet and future generations.

The Significance of Individual Actions

While the scale of climate change may seem overwhelming, it is essential to recognize that every action we take as individuals has an impact, no matter how small. Whether it's reducing our carbon footprint by reducing our energy usage, reducing our consumption and altering our buying habits, minimizing waste, or advocating for policy change, each individual has the power to contribute to the collective effort to tackle climate change.

Moreover, individual actions can be powerful examples and

catalysts for more significant and broader change. When others see their friends, family, and neighbors taking steps to reduce their carbon footprint; they are more likely to follow suit, creating a ripple effect that can lead to the widespread adoption of sustainable practices.

Case Studies of Individual Impact

Throughout history, individuals from all walks of life have played critical roles in driving progress on environmental goals. From grassroots activists organizing community clean-up events to scientists and inventors developing innovative technologies to combat climate change, individual actions have been instrumental in advancing progress on the sustainability agenda.

Take, for instance, the POP Movement, an acronym for Protect Our Planet, a global climate initiative primarily driven by youth (learn more at www.thepopmovement.org), which was co-founded by the late Dr. R.K. Pachauri (visit www.rkpachauri.org), former Chairman of the Intergovernmental Panel on Climate Change (2002-2015) who, alongside former Vice President Al Gore was awarded the Nobel Peace Prize in 2007. This movement, described in more detail in subsequent books in this series, underscores the imperative for individual and collective efforts, innovation, and a steadfast commitment to environmental stewardship. Across 129 countries, the POP Movement has inspired over two million young individuals and fostered 431 partnerships, mobilizing masses to take tangible climate action. Youth activists within the POP Movement are at the forefront, spearheading numerous climate projects, capacity-building endeavors, and educational campaigns worldwide (please visit https://thepopmovement.org/projects/ for more information). However, these endeavors represent only a fraction of the comprehensive response required to mitigate our planet's peril. As aptly expressed by the late Dr. R.K. Pachauri, "Nobody on this planet is going to be untouched by the impacts of climate change." Hence, the POP Movement urgently beckons all global citizens to rally together, leveraging the power of community, knowledge, and diversity to safeguard our planet for future generations.

Overcoming Psychological Barriers

While the potential for individual action to make a significant difference, as witnessed by the POP Movement and other initiatives, is vast and critical, many people confront psychological barriers that prevent them from addressing climate change. These barriers may include feelings of helplessness, anxiety, denial, or apathy, as well as concerns about the perceived inconvenience or cost of adopting sustainable behaviors.

Overcoming these barriers requires a shift in mindset, changes in lifestyle and behavior, and a recognition of the interconnectedness of individual actions and their collective impact. By reframing climate change as an opportunity for positive change rather than an insurmountable challenge, individuals can empower themselves to take meaningful action and inspire others to do the same.

Conclusion

In conclusion, the power of individual action must be balanced when addressing climate change. By recognizing our capacity to make a difference and taking proactive steps to reduce our environmental impact, each one of us has the potential to contribute to building a sustainable future. In the following chapters, we will explore practical strategies for individuals to take action on climate change in their everyday lives.

3

Reducing Carbon Footprint

I ntroduction
One highly impactful approach to addressing climate change involves individuals lowering their carbon footprint. A carbon footprint represents the collective greenhouse gas emissions directly or indirectly generated by a person, entity, product, or occasion. This chapter will delve into practical methods for individuals to shrink their carbon footprint, thereby reducing carbon emissions and resulting environmental impact.

Practical Strategies for Energy Efficiency

1. Home Energy Conservation

Improve Insulation: Proper building and home insulation can significantly reduce carbon emissions and heating and cooling costs by minimizing heat loss in the winter and heat gain in the summer.

Upgrade to Energy-efficient Appliances: Replace old, inefficient appliances with ENERGY STAR-certified appliances that use less energy and reduce greenhouse gas emissions.

Use Programmable Thermostats: Programmable thermostats allow individuals to automatically adjust temperature settings, saving energy when they are away or asleep.

Switch off Lights: Switching off lights when unnecessary is a simple yet effective way to reduce energy consumption.

Here are some tips to make it easier:

a. Install Sensors: Consider installing motion or occupancy sensors in rooms where lights are frequently left on. These sensors can automatically turn off lights when no one is in the room.

b. Use Timers: Set timers for lights in areas where lights may be left on when not in use, such as outdoor lights or lights in common areas.

c. Natural Light: Make the most of natural light during the day by keeping curtains and blinds open. This can reduce the need for artificial lighting. Also, arranging living space and furniture to make the most of natural light during the day can reduce the need for artificial lighting.

d. Switch to LED Bulbs: LED bulbs consume significantly less energy than traditional incandescent bulbs. They also last longer, saving money in the long run.

e. Educate Household Members: Encourage everyone in your household to be mindful of turning off lights when leaving a room. Developing the habit may take some time, but it can greatly affect energy savings.

f. Designated Switches: Designate specific switches for groups of lights to make it easier to turn off multiple lights at once when leaving a room.

g. Regular Maintenance: Ensure that light fixtures and bulbs are well-maintained. Clean fixtures and dust-free bulbs can distribute light more effectively, reducing the need for additional lighting.

h. Disconnect Unused Devices: Disconnect or unplug devices and gadgets not currently in use to minimize unnecessary power consumption and energy usage.

By implementing these simple practices, individuals can contribute to reducing energy consumption and lowering electricity bills.

2. Renewable Energy Sources

Install Solar Panels: Generating electricity from solar panels reduces reliance on fossil fuels and lowers greenhouse gas emissions associated with electricity production.

Green Design and Architecture: Green homes and buildings are designed and constructed sustainably. One aspect is often integrating renewable energy sources into the design and infrastructure.

Here's how green buildings can tap into renewable energy:

a. Solar Power: As mentioned above, installing solar panels on rooftops or building facades is one of the most common ways for green buildings to tap into renewable energy. Solar photovoltaic (PV) systems convert sunlight into electricity, providing a clean and sustainable power source.

b. Wind Power: In some locations, wind turbines can be integrated into the design of green buildings to harness wind energy. However, this is more common in commercial or industrial buildings with ample space for turbine installation.

c. Geothermal Energy: Green buildings can utilize geothermal heat pumps to tap into the Earth's stable underground temperatures for heating and cooling. Geothermal systems are highly efficient and can significantly reduce a home or building's energy consumption and carbon footprint.

d. Biomass Energy: Biomass energy, derived from organic materials such as wood, agricultural residues, or organic waste, can be used for heating or electricity generation in green buildings. Biomass boilers or biogas digesters can be installed to harness this renewable energy source.

e. Hydropower: While less common for individual buildings, hydropower can be utilized in specific locations with access to flowing water. Micro-hydro systems can generate electricity for on-site use or feed excess power back into the grid.

f. Combined Heat and Power (CHP): Also known as cogeneration, CHP systems simultaneously generate electricity and heat from a single fuel source, such as natural gas or biomass. Green buildings can incorporate CHP systems to maximize energy efficiency and reduce reliance on grid-supplied electricity.

g. Passive Design Strategies: In addition to active renewable energy systems, green buildings can employ passive design strategies to optimize energy efficiency. These include orientation to maximize natural light and ventilation, high-performance insulation, and thermal mass to regulate indoor temperatures.

By tapping into renewable energy sources, green buildings reduce their environmental impact and often achieve long-term cost savings through reduced energy costs and increased resilience to energy price fluctuations.

3. Transportation Options

Choose Sustainable Modes of Transportation: To reduce reliance on fossil fuel-powered vehicles, walk, bike, carpool, or use public transport whenever possible.

Drive Fuel-efficient Vehicles: When purchasing a new car, choose a fuel-efficient option with low emissions or consider transitioning to an electric or hybrid vehicle.

4. Refuse, Reduce, Reuse, Recycle

While reducing, reusing, and recycling is effective in reducing an individual's environmental footprint, considering the challenges associated with recycling, particularly in the case of plastic, it's advisable to give precedence to refusing, reducing, and reusing. For example, opting out of single-use plastic straws is an effective individual action.

Minimize Waste Generation: Reduce consumption of single-use products and opt for reusable alternatives whenever possible.

Recycle Responsibly: Properly recycle paper, glass, plastic, and metal materials to conserve resources and reduce greenhouse gas emissions associated with landfilling and incineration.

Proper waste management is crucial in promoting sustainability in several ways, as described below:

a. Resource Conservation: Effective waste management facilitates the recovery and recycling of resources, such as metals, paper, and plastic.

b. Reduced Environmental Impact: Proper waste management minimizes pollution and environmental degradation by controlling the release of harmful substances into the air, water, and soil. This helps protect ecosystems and preserve biodiversity.

c. Energy Recovery: Some waste management practices, such as waste-to-energy facilities and anaerobic digestion, can convert organic waste into renewable energy sources, contributing to the transition to a low-carbon economy and reducing reliance on fossil fuels.

d. Mitigating Climate Change: Waste management can significantly reduce greenhouse gas emissions by diverting organic waste from landfills and utilizing methane capture technologies, thus mitigating climate change impacts.

e. Promoting a Circular Economy: Waste management systems that prioritize recycling, composting, and product reuse contribute to the principles of a circular economy by keeping materials in use for as long as possible, minimizing waste generation, and fostering resource efficiency.

f. Contributing to Community Health and Well-being: Proper waste management practices improve public health by reducing exposure to hazardous materials and preventing the spread of diseases associated with improperly disposed waste.

Effective waste management strategies are essential for achieving sustainability goals by conserving resources, protecting the environment, mitigating climate change, and enhancing community well-being.

5. Dietary Choices and Carbon Emissions

Reduce Meat Consumption: Livestock farming, particularly beef and lamb, is a significant source of methane emissions and requires large amounts of land and water resources. Choosing a plant-based or vegetarian diet or reducing meat consumption can significantly reduce an individual's carbon footprint.

Choose Sustainably Sourced Seafood: Overfishing and unsustainable fishing practices contribute to habitat destruction and biodiversity loss. Choose sustainably sourced seafood options certified by organizations such as the Marine Stewardship Council (MSC) or Seafood Watch.

Support Local and Organic Agriculture: Choosing locally grown and organic produce reduces the carbon emissions of transportation, refrigeration, synthetic fertilizers, and pesticides.

Minimize Food Waste: Approximately one-third of all food produced globally is wasted, contributing to greenhouse gas emissions from landfills. Minimize food waste by planning meals, storing food properly, and composting organic waste.

By implementing these strategies, individuals can significantly reduce their carbon footprint and contribute to the collective effort to combat climate change. Additionally, reducing energy consumption and transitioning to renewable energy sources can lead to cost savings, improve air quality, and create a more sustainable future for future generations.

Conclusion

In conclusion, reducing the individual carbon footprint is essential for mitigating the impacts of climate change and transitioning to a more sustainable society. Individuals can play a vital role in addressing climate change by adopting energy-efficient practices, transitioning to renewable energy sources, making conscious choices about transportation and consumption habits, and altering diets. In the following chapters, we will explore ways individuals can take action to promote sustainability and environmental preservation.

4

Sustainable Consumption

Introduction
Consumer choices significantly impact the environment, from the products that individuals buy to how waste is managed and disposed. Sustainable consumption involves making choices that minimize environmental impact, conserve resources, and promote social equity. This chapter will explore how individuals can adopt sustainable consumption behaviors to reduce their ecological footprint and contribute to a more sustainable planet.

Understanding Environmental Impact

Before making purchasing and consumption decisions, it's essential to understand the environmental impact of individual product and service choices. This includes considering resource extraction, manufacturing processes, transportation, the use phase, and end-of-life product disposal. Individuals can minimize their contribution to pollution, resource depletion, and habitat destruction by choosing products with lower environmental footprints.

Principles of Sustainable Consumption

1. Reduce Consumption

Practice Minimalism: Simplify your lifestyle by decluttering and focusing on experiences rather than material possessions.

Avoid Impulse Buying: Consider whether it is necessary and aligns with your values and sustainability goals before purchasing an item.

2. Choose Sustainable Products

Look for Eco-labels and Certifications: Choose products certified by reputable organizations such as Fair Trade. Choose locally sourced organic products to ensure that they meet environmental and social standards.

Consider the Product's Lifecycle: Choose durable, repairable, and recyclable products to minimize waste and resource consumption.

3. Support Sustainable Brands

Research Companies' Sustainability Practices. Support brands that prioritize environmental stewardship, ethical labor practices, and transparency in their supply chains.

Consider the Social Impact: Choose products from companies that support fair wages, worker rights, and community development initiatives.

4. Reduce Waste

Practice the 4Rs: Refuse, reduce, reuse, recycle. Minimize waste generation by refusing products and choosing products with minimal packaging, reusing items whenever possible, and recycling materials that cannot be avoided.

Compost Organic Waste: Composting food scraps and yard waste reduces methane emissions from landfills and produces nutrient-rich soil for gardening.

5. Promote Circular Economy

Choose Products with Circular Design Principles: Support products and businesses that embrace circular economy principles, such as designing products for durability, repairability, and recyclability.

Participate in Sharing and Rental Platforms: Reduce resource consumption by sharing or renting items such as tools, clothes, and electronics instead of purchasing new ones.

By adopting principles of sustainable consumption, individuals can reduce their ecological footprint, conserve natural resources, and promote a more equitable and sustainable economy. Through informed choices and responsible consumption habits, individuals can contribute to a brighter future for both people and the planet.

Conclusion

In conclusion, sustainable consumption is essential for addressing environmental challenges such as climate change, resource depletion, and pollution. By adopting the principles of refuse, reduce, reuse, and recycle and supporting sustainable brands and products, individuals can minimize their environmental impact and contribute to the transition to a more sustainable society. In the following chapters, we will explore ways individuals can take action to promote sustainability in their daily lives and communities.

5

Advocacy and Community Engagement

I ntroduction
While individual actions are essential, collective efforts
are needed to address systemic issues such as climate
change. Advocacy and community engagement are crucial
in driving policy change, mobilizing resources, and fostering
collaboration to address environmental challenges. In this
chapter, we will explore strategies for individuals to become
advocates for climate action and engage with their communities
to promote sustainability.

Understanding Advocacy
Advocacy involves speaking up for a cause, raising awareness
about issues, and influencing policy decision-makers to take
action. Climate advocacy encompasses various activities, from
grassroots organizing and community outreach to lobbying
policymakers and participating in public discourse. By engaging in advocacy, individuals can magnify community action and
amplify their voices about affecting change at local, national,

and global levels.

Strategies for Climate Advocacy

1. Educate Yourself

Stay informed about climate science, policy developments, and advocacy opportunities through reputable and credible sources such as scientific journals, accurate news outlets, and environmental organizations.

Educate others through conversations, publications, presentations, and social media about the impacts of climate change and the urgency of taking action.

2. Engage with Policymakers

Contact Elected Officials: Write letters, emails, or phone your representatives urging them to support policies that address climate change, such as renewable energy incentives, carbon pricing, and emission reduction targets.

Attend Town Hall Meetings and Public Hearings: Participate in public forums to voice your concerns about climate change and advocate for policy solutions.

3. Mobilize Your Community

Organize Events and Workshops: Host educational events, film screenings, dialogue, and workshops to raise awareness about climate change and empower others to take action.

Build Coalitions: Collaborate with local organizations, businesses, and community groups to coordinate collective action on climate issues and amplify your impact. Demand urgent action from elected officials and only elect representatives who support climate-friendly policies.

4. Support Climate Justice

Center Equity and Justice: Advocate for climate policies that prioritize the needs of marginalized communities and address the disproportionate impacts of climate change on the most vulnerable populations that have contributed the least to the issue of climate change.

Amplify Diverse Voices: Elevate the voices of communities and indigenous peoples directly impacted by climate change and at the frontline of environmental injustice.

5. Use Individual Influence

Use Individual Platform/s: As an influencer, business leader, investor, consumer, or community organizer, leverage individual influence to raise awareness about climate change and promote sustainable practices. Promote demand for sustainable products, services, and supply chains. Support green and clean businesses. Vote into power officials who support sustainable practices and environmental action.

Support Divestment: Advocate for divestment from fossil fuels and investment in renewable energy and sustainable initiatives within your workplace, community, home, or school.

Individuals can drive meaningful change and contribute to collective efforts to address climate change and promote sustainability by engaging in advocacy and community engagement. Individuals can build a more resilient and equitable future for all through collaboration, education, and action.

Conclusion

In conclusion, advocacy and community engagement are essential for addressing climate change and fostering sustainable development. Advocating for policy change, mobilizing resources, and empowering communities can be crucial in driving systemic change and building a more sustainable future. In the following chapters, we will explore ways individuals can take action to promote environmental stewardship and create positive change in their communities.

6

Investing in the Future

I ntroduction
Investing in sustainability is not just about protecting the environment, it's also about securing a more prosperous and equitable future for future generations. This chapter will explore how individuals can align their financial decisions with their values by investing in companies and initiatives that promote environmental action, social responsibility, and long-term sustainability.

Understanding Sustainable Investment

Sustainable investment, also known as socially responsible investing or Environmental, Social, and Governance (ESG) investing, involves considering environmental, social, and governance factors alongside financial returns when making investment decisions. By investing in companies with strong ESG practices, individuals can support businesses prioritizing sustainability and responsible business practices.

Strategies for Sustainable Investing

1. Research Sustainable Investment Options

Explore ESG Funds: Invest in mutual funds, exchange-traded funds (ETFs), or index funds that integrate ESG criteria into their investment strategies.

Consider Impact Investing: Direct your investments towards projects and companies that generate positive social and environmental outcomes, such as renewable energy, clean technology, or sustainable agriculture.

2. Divest from Fossil Fuels

Avoid Investments in Fossil Fuel Companies: Divest from companies involved in the extraction, production, or distribution of fossil fuels, such as coal, oil, and natural gas.

Support Renewable Energy: Invest in companies that develop and deploy renewable energy technologies, such as solar, wind, and hydropower.

3. Engage with Companies

Vote Your Shares: Exercise your shareholder voting rights to support resolutions that promote sustainability, transparency, and accountability within companies.

Engage in Shareholder Activism: Advocate for corporate policies and practices that align with sustainability goals by engaging with company management and participating in shareholder meetings.

4. Consider Long-Term Value

Assess Risks and Opportunities: Evaluate companies based on their long-term sustainability performance, including environmental action, social impact, and governance practices.

Look Beyond Immediate Financial Returns: Consider your investments' broader societal and environmental impacts and potential to generate positive change over the long term.

5. Support Sustainable Finance Initiatives

Invest in Green Bonds: Purchase bonds to finance environmental projects, such as renewable energy infrastructure, energy efficiency retrofits, or sustainable transportation initiatives.

Explore Community Investing: Support community development initiatives, affordable housing projects, and small businesses through community development financial institutions or impact investing platforms.

By incorporating sustainability into investment decisions, individuals can achieve financial goals and contribute to positive social and environmental outcomes. Through conscious investing, individuals have the power to drive capital toward businesses and initiatives that prioritize sustainability and create value for society.

Conclusion

In conclusion, investing in sustainability is a powerful way for individuals to align their financial resources with their values and contribute to positive social and environmental change. By integrating environmental, social, and governance factors into investment decisions, individuals can support businesses that prioritize sustainability and drive positive change. In the following chapters, we will explore ways individuals can take action to promote sustainability and create a more resilient future for all.

7

Education and Awareness

I ntroduction
Education and awareness are crucial in promoting
climate action and supporting sustainability. By increasing
environmental literacy, raising awareness about the impacts of
human activities on the planet, and empowering individuals
to take knowledge-inspired climate action, we can create a
more informed, inspired, and engaged society. In this chapter,
we will explore the importance of education and awareness
in the context of climate action and provide strategies for
promoting environmental literacy in schools, workplaces, and
communities.

The Importance of Environmental Education
Environmental education provides individuals with the
knowledge, skills, and attitudes to understand and address
complex environmental issues such as climate change. By
integrating ecological topics into formal education curricula
and informal learning experiences, we can equip future
generations with the tools they need to become responsible

citizens of the planet who exercise sustainable practices irrespective of their field of specialization or work.

Strategies for Promoting Environmental Education

1. Integrate Environmental Topics into Education Curricula

Incorporate the science of climate change and sustainability activities into school curricula at all levels, from elementary to higher education, across various subjects, including science, social studies, and civics.

Provide hands-on learning experiences such as outdoor education, field trips, and environmental projects to engage students in real-world environmental issues and solutions.

2. Teacher Training and Professional Development

Offer training and resources for educators to enhance their knowledge and teaching skills in environmental education and sustainability.

Provide opportunities for educators to collaborate, share best practices, and develop interdisciplinary curriculum materials that integrate environmental topics into existing lesson plans.

3. Promote Environmental Literacy in the Workplace

Offer environmental awareness training and sustainability workshops to employees to increase their awareness of their work's environmental impact and promote sustainable workplace practices.

Encourage employee engagement in sustainability initiatives such as energy conservation, consumption habits, waste reduction, and green commuting options.

4. Community Outreach and Engagement

Partner with local organizations, non-profits, and government agencies to host community events, workshops, and educational programs on environmental topics such as climate change, recycling, and sustainable living. Help communities understand the implications of unsustainable consumption and production on human health, economy, and security.

Foster collaboration and networking among community members, businesses, and government stakeholders to develop collective solutions to environmental challenges.

5. Use Digital and Media Platforms

Utilize digital platforms, social media, media, and multimedia resources to disseminate information, raise awareness, advocate, and engage audiences in environmental issues and solutions.

Create educational content such as videos, podcasts, infographics, and online courses to reach diverse audiences and inspire climate action and sustainability.

By promoting environmental education and awareness, we can empower individuals to make informed decisions, adopt sustainable behaviors, consume sustainably, and become agents of positive change in their communities and beyond. Through collaborative efforts across sectors, we can build a more environmentally literate and resilient society capable of addressing the challenges of climate change and creating a sustainable future for all.

Conclusion

In conclusion, education and awareness are essential pillars of effective climate action and environmental sustainability. By prioritizing ecological education in schools, workplaces, and communities, we can cultivate a culture of change and empower individuals to impact the planet positively. In the chapters that follow, we will explore additional ways individuals and communities can take action to promote environmental literacy and create a sustainable future.

8

Building Resilience

Introduction

As the impacts of climate change have become increasingly evident, building resilience has become a critical priority for communities worldwide. Resilience involves the ability to anticipate, prepare for, and adapt to the challenges posed by a changing climate while minimizing vulnerability and promoting sustainability. In this chapter, we will explore strategies for building resilience at the individual, community, and societal levels to mitigate the impacts of climate change and foster adaptation.

Understanding Climate Resilience

Climate resilience encompasses a range of strategies and approaches to reduce communities' and ecosystems' vulnerability to climate-related hazards such as extreme weather events, sea-level rise, and shifting precipitation patterns. By building resilience, communities can better withstand and recover from the impacts of climate change while also promoting long-term sustainability and well-being.

Strategies for Building Resilience

1. Risk Assessment and Planning

Conduct Vulnerability Assessments: Identify areas and populations most at risk of climate change impacts, such as coastal communities, low-lying areas, and regions prone to droughts or wildfires.

Develop Climate Adaptation Plans: Collaborate with communities and stakeholders to develop comprehensive adaptation plans that prioritize actions to reduce vulnerability, enhance resilience, and promote sustainable development.

2. Infrastructure and Design

Invest in Resilient Infrastructure: Upgrade and retrofit critical infrastructure such as transportation networks, water and wastewater systems, and energy grids to withstand climate-related hazards, including extreme heatwaves, wildfires, and flooding.

Incorporate Green Infrastructure: Integrate nature-based solutions such as green roofs, permeable pavements, and restored wetlands to manage stormwater, reduce flooding, and enhance biodiversity.

3. Community Engagement and Empowerment

Foster Community Resilience: Engage with community members to identify local priorities, strengths, and vulnerabilities, and empower them to participate in resilience-building efforts and take ownership of their actions by leading them.

Support Social Cohesion: Strengthen social networks, community connections, and mutual aid networks to enhance resilience and promote collective action in response to climate impacts.

Involve local communities in crafting and executing solutions at the grassroots level, and ensuring that initiatives are tailored to and embraced by the communities they serve. This approach empowers communities to take ownership of local solutions, thus building their capacity for sustained action. As the adage goes, "Give a man a fish, and you feed him for a day. Teach a man to fish, and you feed him for a lifetime."

4. Ecosystem Restoration and Conservation

Protect and Restore Natural Ecosystems: Preserve and restore forests, wetlands, and coastal habitats to enhance their resilience to climate change, sequester carbon, and provide ecosystem services such as flood protection and water purification.

Promote Biodiversity Conservation: Protect biodiversity hotspots and endangered species to maintain ecosystem resilience and adaptability in the face of climate change.

5. Adaptive Governance and Policy

Implement Adaptive Governance Structures: Establish

flexible and inclusive decision-making processes that respond effectively to changing climate conditions, community voices, and evolving community needs.

Integrate Climate Resilience into Policy and Planning: To minimize the risk of climate disasters and promote sustainability, incorporate climate resilience considerations into land use planning, zoning regulations, building codes, and infrastructure investments.

By implementing these strategies, communities can enhance their resilience to climate change, reduce vulnerability, and promote long-term sustainability and well-being. Building resilience requires collaboration, innovation, and a commitment to addressing the root causes of vulnerability while adapting to the challenges posed by a changing climate over time.

Conclusion

In conclusion, building resilience is essential for addressing the impacts of climate change and promoting sustainable development. By investing in risk assessment, infrastructure upgrades, community engagement, ecosystem conservation, and adaptive governance, communities can enhance their capacity to withstand and recover from climate-related hazards. The following chapter will explore ways individuals' actions can impact global communities.

9

The Power of Collective Action

I ntroduction
It's evident now that individual actions are feasible and crucial in addressing the urgent issue of climate change. Furthermore, the cumulative effect of each action, along with its potential to inspire change, holds the promise of propelling a widespread movement of collective action. This collective effort is essential for confronting the systemic challenges of climate change. The power of collective action lies in the ability of individuals, communities, organizations, and governments to come together to tackle shared problems and create positive change. This chapter will explore the importance of cumulative and collective action in addressing climate change, highlight successful initiatives and movements, and discuss how individual actions can contribute to collective efforts for a more sustainable future.

The Interconnectedness of Collective Action
Climate change is a global challenge that requires coordinated action at all levels of society. By working together, individuals,

communities, businesses, and governments can leverage their resources, expertise, and influence to implement more effective, equitable, and sustainable solutions than individual efforts alone. Collective action also fosters solidarity, builds social capital, and creates momentum for change by demonstrating the power of collaboration and cooperation.

Examples of Collective Action

1. Global Climate Movements
Guided by young leaders, the POP Movement has rallied millions worldwide to combat climate change. Through the coordination of educational events, advocacy initiatives, and the implementation of technological solutions, youth within the POP Movement are confronting the climate crisis by focusing on local solutions tailored to and led by the communities themselves. Moreover, they actively advocate with global governments and corporations to enact substantive policy changes.

2. Community Renewable Energy Projects
Community-led renewable energy projects, such as solar co-operatives and wind farms, have empowered local communities to take control of their energy future and transition to clean, renewable power sources. By pooling resources and expertise, communities can reduce energy costs, create local jobs, and reduce greenhouse gas emissions.

3. Divestment Campaigns
Divestment campaigns have urged institutions such as universities, pension funds, and religious organizations to divest

from fossil fuel investments and reinvest in clean energy and sustainable initiatives. By targeting the financial industry, divestment campaigns have helped shift capital away from fossil fuels and towards renewable energy while raising awareness about the economic risks of investing in fossil fuels.

4. International Agreements and Treaties

International agreements such as the Paris Agreement provide frameworks for countries to collaborate to mitigate greenhouse gas emissions, adapt to climate change's impacts, and support developing countries in their efforts to transition to low-carbon economies. International agreements play a crucial role in addressing climate change globally by fostering cooperation and collaboration among nations.

Contributing to Collective Action

While collective action often requires coordination and collaboration among diverse stakeholders, individuals can also be crucial in driving change through their actions, advocacy, and engagement. By participating in community initiatives, supporting grassroots movements, voting for climate-conscious leaders, and advocating for policy change, individuals can contribute to collective efforts to address climate change and create a more sustainable future for all.

Conclusion

In conclusion, the power of collective action is essential for addressing the complex and interconnected challenges posed by climate change. By working together, individuals, communities, organizations, and governments can harness their collective resources, expertise, and influence to implement more effective, equitable, and sustainable solutions than individual efforts alone. In the following section, we will explore additional ways individuals can contribute to collective action and create positive change in their communities and worldwide.

10

Embracing the Challenge

The Way Forward
Addressing climate change requires a concerted effort from all sectors of society, from individuals and communities to governments and businesses. Throughout this guide, we have explored a variety of strategies and actions that individuals can take to make a meaningful impact on climate change and promote sustainability in their daily lives and communities.

From reducing carbon emissions and adopting sustainable consumption habits to advocating for policy change and engaging in collective action, there are countless ways for individuals to contribute to the fight against climate change. By taking action, raising awareness, and inspiring others to join the cause, individuals can become agents of positive change and help build a more sustainable future for future generations.

However, addressing climate change also requires systemic change and collective action on a global scale. While individual actions are necessary, they must be complemented by policy changes, investments in clean energy and infrastructure, and international cooperation to effectively mitigate the impacts of climate change and promote resilience in the face of its consequences.

As we progress, it's crucial to maintain our focus on climate action, amplify the voices of marginalized communities, and collaborate toward building a fairer, more equitable, and sustainable world for everyone. Through individual efforts, we can harness the significant impact of collective action, building upon the momentum of grassroots movements and global initiatives to address the challenges of climate change and forge a better future for ourselves and future generations. Together, our actions can effect change.

The time for action is now; urgency is paramount!

If you found this book helpful, I'd appreciate it if you left a favorable review on Amazon!

11

References

- Anderson, L., & Anderson, L. (2023, December 28). *Revealing the top Tree-Planting nation*. Riveal. https://riveal.pt/revealing-the-top-treeplanting-nation/
- *Answers to: Remote sensing is a example of an ICT application for climate change observation*. (2023, May 3). Class Ace. https://www.classace.io/answers/remote-sensing-is-a-example-of-an-ict-application-for-climate-change-observation
- Charlotte. (2023, May 30). *Book Review: The more or less Definitive Guide to Self-Care*. The Roundtable. https://goroundtable.com/blog/book-review-the-more-or-less-definite-guide-to-self-care/
- *Dr. R.K. Pachauri*. (n.d.). https://www.rkpachauri.org/
- González, B. (2021, November 9). Data management and a custom educational model - key factors in post-COVID university education. *UOC*. https://www.uoc.edu/en/news/2021/304-post-COVID-university
- *Goodwall: the app for Gen Z to level up their skills*. (n.d.).

Goodwall. https://www.goodwall.io/posts/climate-chang
e-refers-to-longterm-ffa0f3e6

- Khadka, C., Upadhyaya, A., Edwards-Jonášová, M., Dhun-
gana, N., Baral, S., & Cudlin, P. (2022). Differential Impact
Analysis for Climate Change Adaptation: A Case Study
from Nepal. *Sustainability, 14*(16), 9825. https://doi.org/1
0.3390/su14169825
- *Mozambicans rebuild after deadly Cyclone Freddy - Mozam-
bique.* (2023, August 16). Relief Web. https://reliefweb.int/
report/mozambique/mozambicans-rebuild-after-deadly-
cyclone-freddy
- Pawar, M. (2023, June 15). *Unlocking entrepreneurial success:
The power of setting clear expectations - Mohit Pawar.com.*
Mohit Pawar.com. https://mohitpawar.com/set-clear-exp
ectations/
- *Sadam jutt's writes.* (2023, July 29). https://www.sadamwri
tes.com/search?updated-max=2023-07-29T09:27:00-07:0
0&max-results=5
- Sayings, F. Q. &. (n.d.). *Top 15 Pachauri Quotes & Sayings.*
https://quotessayings.net/topics/pachauri/
- Schulz, K. B. (2015). Information flooding. *Indiana Law
Review, 48*(3), 755. https://doi.org/10.18060/4806.0011
- *Sunak to announce £15bn green savings bonds.* (2021, June 30).
Good With Money. https://good-with-money.com/2021/
06/30/sunak-to-announce-15bn-green-savings-bonds/
- The POP Movement. (2024, April 29). *Home - the POP
Movement - Protect our Planet (POP), Youth inspired by
knowledge.* https://thepopmovement.org/
- *The world counts.* (n.d.). https://www.theworldcounts.com
/challenges/people-and-poverty/hunger-and-obesity/foo
d-waste-statistics

- *Yash Sinha | Vocal.* (n.d.). Vocal. https://vocal.media/author s/yash-sinha

About the Authors

Dr. Ash Pachauri

Director and Senior Mentor, POP Movement

Dr. Ash Pachauri has a PhD in decision behavior and master's degree in international management. Having worked with McKinsey & Company before pursuing a career in the social development arena, Dr. Pachauri's experience in the fields of public health and sustainable development emerge from a range of initiatives including those of the Bill & Melinda Gates Foundation, the UN, CDC program interventions in the US as well as the POP Movement and the World Sustainable Development Forum, respectively. He is a technical adviser to the World Health Organization on Self-Care global guidelines.

Dr. Pachauri has been engaged with the use of information technology for development. A master trainer in behavior change communications and strategic leadership, Dr. Pachauri has led over 20,000 workshops, events, and activities globally to outreach to youth and communities to promote global health and climate action.

Widely published, winner of the prestigious Overseas Research Scholarship, awarded for advanced studies in the U.K. and recognized for his academic achievements, Dr. Pachauri pursues interests in research and teaching through ongoing collaboration with universities and institutions. He published three books as and contributed to eight books and authored over 35 conference papers and publications. Dr. Pachauri has been recognized by the United Nations for his dedication and leadership in their flagship publication "Portraits of Commitment". In 2021, he was awarded the GlobalMindED Inclusive Leadership Award for action in the field of Energy and Sustainability. He is an Associate Fellow of the World Academy of Art and Science. Dr. Pachauri serves on the Boards and Advisory groups of several organizations worldwide, including the Climate Change Coalition and the Global Union of Scientists for Peace.

Dr. Saroj Pachauri

Director and Climate-Health Mentor, POP Movement
As a public health physician, Dr. Pachauri has been extensively engaged with research on family planning, maternal and child health, sexual and reproductive health and rights, HIV and AIDS, and poverty, gender and youth. In 1996, she joined as Regional Director, South and East Asia, Population Council and established its regional office in New Delhi which she managed until 2014. In 2011, she was awarded the prestigious title of Distinguished Scholar, an honor rarely bestowed.

She worked with the Ford Foundation's New Delhi Office (1983-1994) and supported child survival, women's health, sexual and reproductive health, and HIV and AIDS programs. Before that, she worked with the International Fertility Research Program (IFRP) which was later renamed Family Health International (1971-1975) and the India Fertility Research Programme (1975-1983). She designed and monitored multicentric clinical trials globally to assess the safety and effectiveness of fertility control technologies. During 1962-1971, as faculty of the Departments of Preventive and Social Medicine at the Lady Hardinge Medical College, New Delhi and the Institute of Medicine Sciences, Varanasi, she helped to develop this new discipline.

She has published seven books and contributed chapters to 20 books. She has over 100 publications in peer-reviewed journals and several articles in print media.